BREAKING THE CYCLE

THE *ZERO-VIOLENCE CONFLICT-FREE MODEL* FOR PEACE IN ISRAEL AND PALESTINE

BeeUe NiiEe

Breaking The Cycle: The Zero-Violence Conflict-Free Model for Peace in Israel and Palestine

ISBN **979-8-9897518-3-9** (Paperback)
ISBN **979-8-9897518-2-2** (Hardcover)
Also available in eBook and Audio formats

ResearchOnce, USA

To the journalists who report the news, the ordinary citizens who defy local laws to access and share stories on social media, and to social media organizations for democratizing journalism.

PREFACE

The Israel-Palestine conflict is multifaceted with deep roots in the past. Any lasting solution must employ an integrated approach and require the sincere willingness of all stakeholders to yearn for peace. Several attempts at reconciliation have failed because the complexity of the conflict has been oversimplified, leading to an incomplete solution, and lacking a deliberate plan and investments to sustain the peace. "Breaking the Cycle" offers a roadmap towards a peaceful future for Israel and Palestine.

This book proposes a fresh approach to the resolution of this conflict. It is an attempt to extend the Zero-Violence Conflict-Free Model to resolve one of the most challenging conflicts known to man. The model is designed to create peace in an already tense environment and involves known concepts. The novelty is in the comprehensive approach and method of application.

The Zero-Violence Conflict-Free Model is an integrated approach where all stakeholders' roles are clear. From understanding the causes through negotiation to maintaining the peace, the model emphasizes the transparency that creates an immeasurable affinity for peace among stakeholders. Applying the model to the Israel and Palestine conflict is long overdue. I encourage scholars, experts, governments, international bodies for peace and non-governmental organizations, and especially the citizens of the conflict zones to rise and work for peace between Israel and Palestine.

This book was inspired by the images of war that were broadcast over major networks. I sat glued to the TV and occasional social media feeds where some of the images seemed more gruesome. The ugly faces of war are nondiscriminatory—not by side, not by gender, not by occupation, and not by age. War consumes established communities—all lives, flora, and fauna on its path.

"In war, whichever side may call itself the victor, there are no winners, but all are losers." - *Neville Chamberlain (1869–1940), speech at Kettering, 3 July 1938, in Times 4 July 1938*

To the journalists who risk their lives daily to report the news, and to the ordinary citizens who defy local country laws to access and share stories on social media, thank you! I also extend my gratitude to the social media organizations for democratizing journalism. Your efforts have helped to make the world a more informed and connected place.

BeeUe NiiEe

Table of Contents

CHAPTER 1: UNDERSTANDING THE ISRAEL AND PALESTINIAN CONFLICT

HISTORICAL BACKGROUND OF THE CONFLICT

The Israel and Palestinian conflict is one of the most enduring and complex conflicts in modern history. To fully understand the current state of tension and strive towards creating peace, it is essential to explore the historical background that has shaped the conflict over the years.

The roots of the conflict can be traced back to the late 19th century when Jewish and Arab national movements gained momentum in the region (D.A.S et al., 2023). The Zionist movement, advocating for the establishment of a Jewish homeland, gained traction amongst Jewish communities around the world (Faye, 2023). At the same time, Arab nationalism emerged as a response to fears of losing their political and cultural identity.

In 1947, the United Nations proposed a partition plan that would divide Palestine into separate Jewish and Arab states (Sakib, 2023; Wagiihash, 2023). While many Jews accepted the plan, Arab leaders rejected it, leading to the Arab-Israeli War of 1948 (Historian, 2023). This war resulted in the establishment of the State of Israel and the displacement of hundreds of thousands of Palestinians, creating a deep sense of resentment and injustice.

In the following decades, several wars, uprisings, and peace negotiations took place, each leaving its mark on the conflict. The Six-Day War in 1967 led to Israel's occupation of the West Bank,

Gaza Strip, and East Jerusalem, further exacerbating tensions. The Oslo Accords in the 1990s aimed to establish a framework for peace, but ultimately failed to address the core issues, leading to increased frustration and violence (Staff, 2023).

The recent incursions into the Gaza envelope of neighboring Israeli territory by Hamas-led gunmen launching a coordinated armed attack, resulting in the death of at least 1,400 people, many of them civilians, including children has exacerbated the situation. In response, Israel launched a military operation, vowing to eliminate Hamas. The conflict has had a profound impact on both Israelis and Palestinians. Both sides have experienced loss, trauma, and a deep sense of mistrust. Generations have grown up in an environment of violence and hostility, perpetuating a cycle that seems impossible to break.

ROOT CAUSES OF THE CONFLICT

Understanding the root causes of the Israel-Palestinian conflict is crucial to effectively address and find solutions to this longstanding issue. The conflict, which has spanned decades and claimed countless lives, is deeply rooted in historical, political, and socio-economic factors that have shaped the region. In this subchapter, we will delve into the key root causes that have contributed to the ongoing tensions and violence between Israel and Palestine.

Historical Context:

The historical context of the Israel-Palestinian conflict dates back to the early 20th century, when conflicting national aspirations emerged in the region. The establishment of the State of Israel in 1948 and the subsequent displacement of Palestinians created a deep sense of injustice and resentment, fueling the conflict. The complex history of the region, including the Arab-Israeli wars, the occupation of Palestinian territories, and failed peace negotiations, has further deepened the divide between the two sides.

Political Factors:

Political factors have played a significant role in perpetuating the conflict. The question of borders, the status of Jerusalem, the right of return for Palestinian refugees, and the establishment of a sovereign Palestinian state are among the key political issues that have proven to be major obstacles to peace. In addition, the presence of extremist groups on both sides, such as Hamas and certain Israeli settler movements, have further complicated the path to reconciliation.

Socio-Economic Factors:

Socio-economic factors have also contributed to the conflict. The lack of basic resources, including water and land, has created competition and grievances among Israelis and Palestinians. The unequal distribution of resources, economic disparities, and high unemployment rates have fueled frustration and resentment, amplifying tensions between the two communities.

Religious and Cultural Differences:

Religious and cultural differences have added another layer of complexity to the conflict. The holy sites in Jerusalem, including the Al-Aqsa Mosque and the Western Wall, hold immense significance for both Muslims and Jews, making any compromise on their status highly sensitive. The divergent narratives and historical interpretations of the conflict from both sides have deepened the sense of mistrust and animosity.

The root causes of the Israel-Palestinian conflict are multifaceted and deeply entrenched. Understanding these causes is essential to create sustainable solutions for peace. By addressing historical, political, socio-economic, and religious factors, we can begin to break the cycle of violence and work towards a future that respects the rights and aspirations of both Israelis and Palestinians. The Zero-Violence Conflict-Free Model offers a promising framework for finding common ground and fostering dialogue, ultimately leading to a peaceful resolution in this tense and challenging environment.

CURRENT STATE OF THE CONFLICT

The Israel and Palestinian conflict has been a long-standing issue that has led to significant tension and violence in the region. The situation has become increasingly complex, with both sides entrenched in their positions and a lack of progress in finding a peaceful solution. This subchapter will provide an overview of the current state of the conflict and explore the potential for applying the Zero-Violent- Conflict-Free Model to bring about peace in this tense environment.

The conflict is marked by sporadic outbreaks of violence, territorial disputes, and a lack of trust between the parties involved. The Israeli government continues to build settlements in the occupied territories, which the Palestinians view as a violation of their rights and a hindrance to the establishment of a viable Palestinian state. On the other hand, Israel argues that these settlements are necessary for security and to preserve their historical claims to the land.

At present, there is an ongoing war between Hamas and Israel. On October 7, 2023, Hamas launched a coordinated armed attack, resulting in the death of at least 1,400 people, many of them civilians, including children. In response, Israel launched a military operation, vowing to eliminate Hamas. The conflict has led to several civilian casualties on both sides with no end in sight.

In addition to this territorial dispute, the conflict is also fueled by religious and cultural differences, economic disparities, and a profound lack of understanding between the Israeli and Palestinian people. Both sides have suffered greatly, with countless lives lost and communities torn apart by the violence.

However, amidst this grim reality, there is hope. The Zero-Violence Conflict-Free Model offers a new perspective and a potential pathway towards peace. By emphasizing nonviolent communication, dialogue, and empathy, this model aims to break the cycle of violence and create an environment conducive to peaceful coexistence.

Applying the Zero-Violence Conflict-Free Model to the Israel and Palestinian conflict requires a multi- faceted approach. It involves engaging with all stakeholders, including government officials, religious leaders, civil society organizations, and ordinary citizens, to foster a culture of peace and reconciliation. This approach acknowledges the importance of addressing the root causes of the conflict, such as the need for self-determination, security, and equal rights for all.

Moreover, implementing this model

necessitates the establishment of trust-building mechanisms, such as joint economic projects, educational initiatives, and cultural exchanges. By creating opportunities for cooperation and mutual understanding, the Zero-Violence Conflict-Free Model offers a chance to bridge the divide and pave the way for lasting peace.

The current state of the Israel and Palestinian conflict is marked by deep-seated divisions, violence, and a lack of progress towards a peaceful resolution. However, by applying the Zero-Violence Conflict-Free Model, there is a glimmer of hope for creating peace in this tense environment. By fostering dialogue, empathy, and understanding, this model offers an innovative approach to breaking the cycle of violence and building a future of coexistence and harmony for all ages in the region.

CHAPTER 2: INTRODUCTION TO THE ZERO-VIOLENCE CONFLICT-FREE MODEL

OVERVIEW OF THE MODEL

Amid the ongoing Israel and Palestinian conflict, there is a desperate need for innovative approaches to peacebuilding. "Breaking the Cycle: The Zero-Violence Conflict-Free Model for Peace in Israel and Palestine" presents a groundbreaking solution that is applicable to all ages and aims to create peace in an already tense environment. By applying the Zero-Violence Conflict-Free Model, we can foster reconciliation, understanding, and ultimately pave the way for lasting peace.

The Zero-Violence Conflict-Free Model is based on the idea that violence perpetuates violence, and the only way to break this cycle is by adopting non-violent strategies. This model emphasizes the importance of dialogue, negotiation, and mediation to resolve conflicts and promote peaceful coexistence. It recognizes that peace cannot be achieved through force or domination but requires a mutual understanding and respect for each other's rights and aspirations.

One of the key aspects of this model is the inclusion of all ages in the peacebuilding process. It recognizes that peace is not solely the responsibility of political leaders or diplomats but requires the participation and engagement of individuals from all levels of society. By involving children, youth, adults, and the elderly, we can create a holistic approach to peacebuilding that addresses the needs and concerns of all generations. This inclusivity ensures that peace is not just a distant dream but a reality that is attainable for everyone.

The Zero-Violence Conflict-Free Model also emphasizes the importance of education in promoting peace. Through educational initiatives that teach tolerance, empathy, and conflict resolution skills, we can empower individuals with the tools they need to peacefully resolve disputes. By fostering a culture of peace from an early age, we can break the cycle of violence and create a more harmonious society.

This subchapter will delve into the various components of the Zero-Violence Conflict-Free Model, including the role of dialogue, mediation, and education in promoting peace. We will explore real-life examples of successful peace initiatives that could be implemented in the Israel and Palestinian conflict, highlighting the potential transformative power of this model.

Whether you are a student, a parent, a community leader, or simply someone interested in creating peace in a tense environment, this subchapter will provide you with the knowledge and tools to make a positive impact. By understanding and applying the Zero-Violence Conflict-Free Model, we can break the cycle of violence and build a future of peace in Israel and Palestine.

THE ZERO-VIOLENCE CONFLICT-FREE MODEL

What is the Zero-Violence Conflict-Free Model
The Zero-Violence Conflict-Free Model is a negotiation model that aims to create peace and coexistence between parties in conflict. It was first developed as a listing of need-to-know elements and requirements for a fair negotiation and the peaceful

coexistence of fenceline host communities and multinational corporations in the natural resource extraction industry. The model was first discussed in the book, "Multinational Corporations and Host Communities: Proposing the Zero-Violent Conflict Model." (Yorgure, 2016).

Extending the Zero-Violence Conflict-Free Model

The Zero-Violence Conflict-Free Model is a negotiation model that can be applied to conflicts of any scale. The model relies on a series of negotiations where competent and teams fairly represent each party. Mediator(s) are crucial in complex cases; it is not a requirement for this model. The hallmarks of the model are inclusive representation, understanding of each party's intentions and demands, the demand overlaps, and the categorization of each demand into critical and noncritical to acceptance peace factors, negotiate, and maintain the peace.

The following elements are essential to successfully operationalize the model:

- Gather the data—document the cause of conflict and potential peace factors.

- Negotiate—Noncritical to Acceptance Peace Factors (NCTAPFs) and Critical to Acceptance Peace Factors (CTAPFs)

- Create Final Peace Contract Document (FPCDoc).

- Maintain the peace

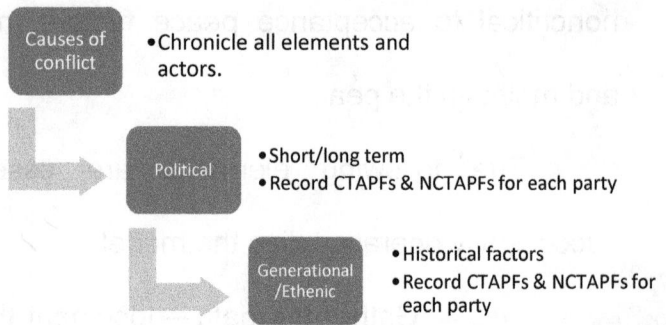

Figure 1: Data elements

Negotiation strategy

The negotiation strategy begins by tabulating CTAPFs (Critical to Acceptance Peace Factors) and NCTAPFs (Noncritical to Acceptance Peace Factors). These factors are subject to change over time and require regular updates. The objective is to have each party drop what they consider critical demands or come to a point of compromise. The negotiators offer the NCTAPFs of one party in exchange for the second party's CTAPFs. If successful, Party A gives up its CTAPFs for the NCTAPFs of Party B, and vice versa. The shifts on CTAPFs and NCTAPFs become inputs to the FPCDoc (Final Peace Contract Document).

Public campaigns may be required to sway public opinion. Press/media sympathetic to the cause on each side may be identified for relentless publicity, each pushing the desired opinion in a predetermined direction.

Maintain the Peace

Peace is fragile at all phases, more so, when freshly achieved. Design socio-economic programs to nurture peace, foster unity, and to further bring the people together. The following are examples of programs to sustain the peace:

- Economic programs
  - Industrial development programs
  - Technical Development

programs

- Educational exchange programs
- Youth social programs—sports, etc.
  - o Reach the youths at the very bottom of the rungs— friendships cultivated at early ages hardly falter; they are reliable vehicles of unity.

PRINCIPLES AND VALUES OF THE MODEL

In the quest for peace in the Israel and Palestinian conflict, it is essential to establish a solid foundation built upon principles and values that can guide us towards a sustainable and lasting resolution. The Zero-Violence Conflict-Free Model offers a unique approach that aims to break the cycle of violence and build a harmonious coexistence between Israelis and Palestinians. This subchapter will delve into the core principles and values that underpin this transformative model.

Primarily, the model emphasizes the importance of dialogue and understanding. It recognizes that true peace can only be achieved through open and honest communication between the conflicting parties. By creating safe spaces for dialogue, both sides can express their concerns, fears, and aspirations, fostering empathy and building bridges of understanding.

Another crucial principle of the model is the promotion of non-violence and the rejection of any form of aggression or hostility. It acknowledges that violence only perpetuates the cycle of conflict and deepens the wounds inflicted upon both Israelis and Palestinians. Instead, the model encourages alternative means of conflict resolution, such as negotiation, mediation, and diplomacy, to resolve disputes and grievances.

The model also emphasizes the importance of inclusivity and equality. It recognizes that peace cannot be achieved by marginalizing or excluding any group. Instead, it advocates for equal participation and representation of all stakeholders, regardless of their religious, ethnic, or cultural background. By ensuring that all voices are heard and respected, the model aims to foster a sense of ownership and shared responsibility for peacebuilding.

Furthermore, the model places great emphasis on education and youth empowerment. It recognizes the pivotal role that education plays in shaping future generations and breaking the cycle of violence. By promoting peace education in schools and providing opportunities for youth engagement in peacebuilding initiatives, the model seeks to cultivate a culture of peace from an early age and empower young people to become agents of change.

Lastly, the model highlights the importance of international cooperation and support. It acknowledges that the Israel and Palestinian conflict is not isolated, and that the global community has a responsibility to contribute to its resolution. By fostering international partnerships and leveraging resources, the model aims to create an enabling environment for peacebuilding efforts, ensuring the sustainability and success of the proposed solutions.

The principles and values of the Zero-Violence Conflict-Free Model provide a roadmap for creating peace in the tense environment of the Israel and Palestinian conflict. Through dialogue, non- violence, inclusivity, education, and international cooperation, this model offers an integrated approach that can pave the way towards a harmonious coexistence and a brighter future for all ages in the region.

THEORETICAL FOUNDATIONS OF THE MODEL

To create peace in an already tense environment, it is essential to have a solid theoretical framework on which to build a model. The Zero-Violence Conflict-Free Model for Peace in Israel and Palestine is built upon a comprehensive understanding of conflict resolution and peacebuilding theories. This subchapter will explore the theoretical foundations of the model, providing readers of all ages with a deeper insight into the principles and concepts that underpin this innovative approach.

At the heart of the model is the belief that

violence can never be a solution to any conflict. This principle draws heavily from the Gandhian philosophy of nonviolence, which emphasizes the power of peaceful resistance and the ability to resolve conflicts through dialogue and mutual understanding. By rejecting violence as a means to an end, the model aims to create a sustainable and lasting peace in the Israel and Palestinian conflict.

Furthermore, the model draws inspiration from various other theoretical frameworks, including transformative mediation and conflict transformation. Transformative mediation focuses on empowering individuals to take ownership of their conflicts and find mutually beneficial solutions. Conflict transformation, on the other hand, seeks to address the root causes of the conflict and transform relationships, structures, and attitudes that perpetuate violence.

The Zero-Violence Conflict-Free Model also incorporates elements of positive peace, which goes beyond the mere absence of violence and strives to create a society that is just, inclusive, and equitable. By promoting social justice, human rights, and equality, the model aims to address the underlying grievances and inequalities that fuel the conflict.

Another important theoretical foundation of the model is the concept of dialogue and communication. Drawing from the work of renowned peacebuilders such as John Paul Lederach (Pillay, 2006; Pointer, 2021), the model emphasizes the importance of fostering open and honest dialogue between conflicting parties. By creating spaces for dialogue and facilitating constructive conversations, the model aims to build trust, understanding, and empathy among individuals and communities.

Overall, the theoretical foundations of the Zero-Violence Conflict-Free Model provide a comprehensive framework for creating peace in the Israel and Palestinian conflict. By drawing from various theories of conflict resolution, nonviolence, and peacebuilding, the model offers a comprehensive approach that addresses the root causes of the conflict and fosters sustainable peace. Understanding these theoretical foundations is crucial for anyone interested in applying the model and contributing to the creation of peace in this tense environment.

CHAPTER 3: APPLYING THE ZERO-VIOLENCE CONFLICT-FREE MODEL TO ISRAEL AND PALESTINE

CHALLENGES AND OPPORTUNITIES IN THE ISRAEL AND PALESTINIAN CONTEXT

In the complex and deeply rooted conflict between Israel and Palestine, numerous challenges and opportunities arise in the pursuit of peace. This subchapter delves into the unique dynamics of the Israeli and Palestinian context, exploring the obstacles that hinder progress while also highlighting the potential avenues for resolution. By applying the Zero-Violence Conflict-Free Model, we can unlock the transformative power of peacebuilding and work towards lasting reconciliation.

One of the foremost challenges in this

conflict is the deep-seated mistrust between the Israeli and Palestinian populations. Decades of violence, historical grievances, and political disagreements have fueled this animosity, making it difficult to establish a common ground for negotiations. Additionally, the divided nature of the Israeli and Palestinian leadership, with differing agendas and priorities, has hindered the development of a cohesive peace process.

Another significant challenge lies in the geographical and territorial disputes. The Israeli settlements in the West Bank, the status of Jerusalem, and the right of return for Palestinian refugees are all contentious issues that have fueled tensions for years. Resolving these territorial disputes requires delicate negotiations and compromises from both sides, which have proven elusive thus far.

Nevertheless, within these challenges, opportunities for peace exist. The shared desire for security and a better future for both Israelis and Palestinians can serve as a foundation for building trust and cooperation. The younger generation, in particular, offers hope for a new approach, as they are more open-minded and willing to engage in dialogue.

Furthermore, economic cooperation and development can provide a path towards peace. By promoting trade and investment between Israeli and Palestinian businesses, both parties can experience the benefits of mutual prosperity. This economic interdependence can foster a sense of shared interests and reduce the incentive for violence.

Education and grassroots initiatives also play a vital role in fostering peace. By promoting intercultural understanding, empathy, and tolerance, we can challenge the narratives of hate and division that perpetuate the conflict. Through educational programs, joint projects, and people-to-people interactions, Israelis and Palestinians can develop a deeper understanding of each other's perspectives and build bridges of trust.

The Israeli and Palestinian context presents unique challenges and opportunities for peacebuilding. By applying the Zero-Violence Conflict-Free Model, we can address the deep-rooted mistrust, territorial disputes, and other obstacles that hinder progress towards peace. Through trust- building measures, economic cooperation, and educational initiatives, we can lay the foundation for a more peaceful and harmonious future for both Israelis and Palestinians. It is through our collective efforts and dedication to breaking the cycle of violence that we can truly transform the Israeli and Palestinian conflict.

ENGAGING KEY STAKEHOLDERS IN THE PEACE PROCESS

One of the fundamental aspects of achieving lasting peace in any conflict-ridden region is the active involvement of key stakeholders. In the context of the Israel and Palestinian conflict, engaging these stakeholders becomes even more crucial due to the deep-rooted tensions and complexities involved. This subchapter explores the significance of engaging key stakeholders and how it can contribute to the successful implementation of the Zero-Violence Conflict-Free Model for peace in Israel and Palestine.

Key stakeholders in this conflict include

political leaders, community representatives, religious figures, and international mediators. Each stakeholder group brings a unique perspective and set of interests to the table, making their engagement essential for any peace process. By involving these stakeholders, the peace process gains legitimacy and widens its scope, ensuring that the concerns and aspirations of all parties are heard and addressed.

Engaging stakeholders also fosters a sense of ownership and responsibility among those involved. When individuals feel that their voices are being heard and their opinions matter (Hu & Han, 2023), they are more likely to actively participate in the peace process and commit to its success. This sense of ownership can be cultivated through various means, such as inclusive dialogue sessions, community forums, and participatory decision-making processes. These platforms provide opportunities for stakeholders to voice their concerns, express their grievances, and propose solutions, thus promoting a sense of empowerment and collective responsibility.

Furthermore, engaging key stakeholders enables the identification of shared interests and common ground. Despite the deeply entrenched divisions, there are often areas where the interests of different stakeholder groups overlap. By focusing on these shared interests, the peace process can build bridges and create a foundation for cooperation. This requires open and honest dialogue, where each party listens to the perspectives of others and seeks to understand their underlying motivations and needs.

Engaging key stakeholders is vital for the success of any peace process, particularly in the context of the Israel and Palestinian conflict. By involving political leaders, community representatives, religious figures, and international mediators, the peace process gains legitimacy, fosters a sense of ownership, and identifies shared interests. It is through these inclusive and participatory approaches that the Zero-Violence Conflict-Free Model can be effectively applied to create peace in an already tense environment. Only by coming together and engaging in constructive dialogue can we hope to break the cycle of violence and build a future of harmony and coexistence for all ages.

IMPLEMENTING NON-VIOLENT STRATEGIES FOR CONFLICT RESOLUTION

In a world marred by conflicts and violence, the need for effective strategies to resolve conflicts peacefully has never been more crucial. This subchapter aims to explore the implementation of non- violent strategies for conflict resolution, specifically focusing on the context of the Israel and Palestinian conflict. By applying the Zero-Violence Conflict-Free Model, we can create peace in an already tense environment.

Non-violent strategies offer a powerful alternative to the cycle of violence that has plagued the Israel and Palestinian conflict for decades. By shifting the paradigm from aggression and retaliation to dialogue and understanding, we can pave the way for a sustainable and peaceful resolution. These strategies can be applied by individuals, communities, and governments alike, fostering a culture of peace and cooperation.

One of the key elements of non-violent strategies is the promotion of dialogue and empathy. By encouraging open and honest communication between conflicting parties, we can foster mutual understanding and bridge the gap between different perspectives. This process requires active listening, respecting diverse viewpoints, and acknowledging the emotions and experiences of others. Through dialogue, we can humanize the "other" and recognize our shared humanity, creating a foundation for peaceful coexistence.

Another vital aspect of non-violent strategies is the promotion of education and awareness. By fostering a culture of peace from an early age, we can equip future generations with the necessary skills and knowledge to resolve conflicts non-violently. Education should emphasize the importance of empathy, tolerance, and respect for diversity. By instilling these values in children, we can break the cycle of violence and create a generation committed to peaceful coexistence.

Furthermore, non-violent strategies involve the implementation of tangible actions to address the root causes of the conflict. This includes addressing issues such as economic disparity, access to resources, and political inequalities. By promoting social justice and equality, we can address the underlying grievances that fuel the conflict, creating a more stable and peaceful environment for all.

Implementing non-violent strategies for conflict resolution requires collective effort and commitment from all stakeholders involved. It necessitates a shift in mindset from resorting to violence to resolve conflicts, to embracing non-violent alternatives. By adopting the Zero-Violence Conflict-Free Model, we can break free from the cycle of violence and build a future of peace and harmony in Israel and Palestine.

In conclusion, implementing non-violent strategies for conflict resolution is of paramount importance in creating peace in an already tense environment. By promoting dialogue, fostering education and awareness, and addressing the root causes of the conflict, we can pave the way for a sustainable and peaceful resolution. It is up to all of us, regardless of age, to embrace non-violent strategies and work towards a future free from violence and conflict.

CHAPTER 4: BUILDING TRUST AND MUTUAL UNDERSTANDING

COMMUNICATION AND DIALOGUE TECHNIQUES

Communication and dialogue techniques are essential tools for creating peace in any tense environment, especially in the context of the Israel and Palestinian conflict. In this subchapter, we will explore the principles and strategies of effective communication that can be applied to break the cycle of violence and foster understanding and dialogue between the two sides.

One of the fundamental communication techniques is active listening. Active listening involves not only hearing the words being spoken but also understanding the underlying emotions and perspectives behind them (Interobservers,

2023; Vescio, et al., 2003). By truly listening to each other, both Israelis and Palestinians can begin to empathize with one another's experiences and grievances, laying the foundation for open dialogue.

Another crucial technique is the use of nonviolent language. In a conflict-ridden environment, it is easy for emotions to escalate and for hurtful words to be exchanged. However, by consciously choosing nonviolent and respectful language, individuals can create a safer space for dialogue. This involves reframing statements from blaming and accusatory language to using statements with personal pronouns and expressing feelings and needs.

Furthermore, effective communication involves building trust between the parties involved. Trust is essential for open and honest dialogue to occur. This can be achieved by practicing transparency, keeping commitments, and showing respect for one another's boundaries. By building trust over time, Israelis and Palestinians can establish a solid foundation for meaningful dialogue and conflict resolution.

In addition to these techniques, it is crucial to create a safe and inclusive environment for communication. This may involve providing a neutral space where both sides feel comfortable expressing their thoughts and emotions without fear of judgment or retaliation. Facilitators can also play a significant role in ensuring that the dialogue remains respectful and focused on finding common ground.

Lastly, the use of mediation and negotiation techniques can be instrumental in resolving conflicts. Mediators can help facilitate communication between Israelis and Palestinians and guide them towards finding mutually acceptable solutions. Negotiation techniques such as compromise and finding win-win solutions can also be employed to break the cycle of violence and create a sustainable peace.

In conclusion, communication and dialogue techniques are powerful tools for creating peace in the tense environment of the Israel and Palestinian conflict. By practicing active listening, using nonviolent language, building trust, creating safe spaces, and employing mediation and negotiation techniques, Israelis and Palestinians can move towards a future of understanding, reconciliation, and lasting peace.

PROMOTING EMPATHY AND PERSPECTIVE-TAKING

In the quest for peace in the Israel and Palestinian conflict, one of the most essential elements is the promotion of empathy and perspective-taking. Breaking the Cycle: The Zero-Violence Conflict-Free Model for Peace in Israel and Palestine emphasizes the significance of these qualities in bridging the divide and fostering understanding among the different parties involved. This subchapter explores practical approaches and strategies to promote empathy and perspective-taking, offering hope for a peaceful resolution (Vescio, et al., 2003).

Empathy, the ability to understand and share the feelings of another, is a fundamental aspect of human connection (Travers, 2023). By encouraging individuals from both sides of the conflict to develop empathy, we can begin to break down the barriers that perpetuate violence and hostility. The book advocates for educational programs that focus on teaching empathy from an early age, providing opportunities for children and adults alike to engage in activities that cultivate compassion and understanding. By fostering empathy, the next generation can rise above the cycle of violence and work towards a future of coexistence.

Another crucial element in promoting empathy and perspective-taking is creating spaces for dialogue and interaction between Israelis and Palestinians. Breaking the Cycle emphasizes the need for structured platforms where individuals from both sides can come together to share their stories, fears, and hopes. These spaces provide an opportunity to challenge preconceived notions, dismantle stereotypes, and cultivate a deeper understanding of each other's experiences and perspectives. By engaging in meaningful conversations, individuals can begin to see the humanity in one another, fostering empathy and paving the way towards reconciliation.

Moreover, the subchapter explores the power of storytelling in promoting empathy. By sharing personal narratives, individuals can connect on a deeper level, transcending political divisions and realizing the shared human experience. The book suggests establishing storytelling projects that allow Israelis and Palestinians to share their stories, creating a platform where their voices can be heard and understood. Through these narratives, empathy can be fostered, as individuals gain insight into the struggles and triumphs experienced by those on the other side of the conflict.

Ultimately, promoting empathy and perspective-taking is essential in the pursuit of peace in the Israel and Palestinian conflict. Breaking the Cycle offers practical strategies and approaches to cultivate empathy from an early age, create spaces for dialogue, and harness the power of storytelling. By embracing these principles, individuals of all ages can contribute to the transformation of an already tense environment and work towards a future of peaceful coexistence.

ADDRESSING HISTORICAL GRIEVANCES AND TRAUMA

In the pursuit of peace, it is essential to acknowledge and address the historical grievances and trauma that have plagued the relationship between Israel and Palestine. The decades-long conflict has left deep scars on both sides, resulting in a cycle of violence, mistrust, and animosity. To break this cycle and create lasting peace, it is crucial to confront the historical grievances and trauma head-on.

Historical grievances refer to the deep-rooted feelings of injustice and resentment that arise from past events. In the case of Israel and Palestine, both sides have experienced significant historical grievances. For Israelis, the trauma of the Holocaust and the longing for a homeland after centuries of persecution cannot be understated. Similarly, Palestinians feel the pain of dispossession and displacement, as well as the ongoing impact of occupation and conflict on their daily lives.

To address historical grievances, it is necessary to create spaces for dialogue and reconciliation. This involves acknowledging the past, listening to the narratives of both sides, and fostering empathy and understanding. By providing a platform for individuals to share their experiences and pain, healing can begin.

Trauma, on the other hand, refers to the psychological and emotional wounds inflicted by violence and conflict. The Israel-Palestine conflict has resulted in widespread trauma among both Israelis and Palestinians. From the fear and anxiety of living under constant threat to the grief and loss experienced due to the loss of loved ones, trauma has shaped the lives of countless individuals in the region.

Addressing trauma requires a comprehensive approach that includes providing mental health support, implementing trauma-informed care, and promoting resilience and healing. This involves investing in mental health services, training professionals in trauma treatment, and destigmatizing seeking help for psychological well-being.

The process of addressing historical grievances and trauma is complex and challenging. However, it is a necessary step towards building a foundation for peace. By acknowledging the pain and suffering of both Israelis and Palestinians, we can begin to pave the way for reconciliation, understanding, and a shared vision for a peaceful future.

In conclusion, addressing historical grievances and trauma is a critical aspect of creating peace in an already tense environment like the Israel-Palestinian conflict. By recognizing and validating the experiences of both sides, we can lay the groundwork for healing, understanding, and ultimately, a peaceful coexistence. It is only through confronting the past that we can break the

cycle of violence and build a brighter future for all

generations.

CHAPTER 5: FOSTERING COOPERATION AND COLLABORATION

IDENTIFYING SHARED GOALS AND INTERESTS

In the pursuit of peace, it is crucial to identify shared goals and interests between conflicting parties. This subchapter delves into the importance of recognizing common ground and finding a mutual understanding in the context of the Israel and Palestinian conflict. By applying the Zero-Violence Conflict-Free Model, we can explore ways to create peace in an already tense environment.

Regardless of age, we all have a stake in fostering peace and resolving conflicts that have plagued the region for decades. This subchapter aims to provide a comprehensive understanding of the shared goals and interests that can pave the way for a sustainable resolution.

One of the most powerful tools for identifying shared goals and interests is dialogue. Meaningful conversations create a platform for both parties to express their desires, fears, and aspirations. By engaging in open and respectful dialogue, we can discover the common values and goals that unite us. Whether it is the desire for security, stability, or a better future for our children, finding shared interests can be a catalyst for peacebuilding.

Another crucial aspect of identifying shared goals and interests is recognizing the interdependence of both parties. The Israel and Palestinian conflict is not isolated; it affects the entire region and beyond. This subchapter emphasizes the need to understand the ripple effects of the conflict and how finding common ground can benefit all stakeholders involved.

Moreover, it is essential to focus on the human element of the conflict. Acknowledging the suffering and grievances experienced by individuals on both sides can foster empathy and compassion. By recognizing the shared pain and aspirations for a better future, we can transcend the boundaries that divide us.

This subchapter also highlights the significance of shared economic interests. Economic development and prosperity can be a powerful incentive for peace. By identifying common economic goals, such as trade, tourism, or resource management, we can create a foundation for collaboration and mutual benefit.

Ultimately, identifying shared goals and interests is a crucial step toward resolving the Israel and Palestinian conflict. By engaging in dialogue, recognizing interdependence, focusing on the human element, and embracing economic cooperation, we can lay the groundwork for a peaceful and sustainable future. This subchapter provides valuable insights and strategies for all ages, offering hope for a brighter tomorrow in a region burdened by tension and violence.

CREATING JOINT PROJECTS AND INITIATIVES

Creating joint projects and initiatives is a crucial step towards building peace in an already tense environment. In the context of the Israel and Palestinian conflict, where violence and hostility have dominated for decades, it is essential to find innovative and alternative approaches that can bring about lasting change. This subchapter explores the concept of joint projects and initiatives to foster understanding, collaboration, and ultimately, peace.

Joint projects and initiatives encompass a wide range of activities that bring people from diverse backgrounds together to work towards a common goal. These projects can be in various sectors such as education, healthcare, infrastructure, or environmental conservation. By engaging individuals from both sides of the conflict, joint projects create opportunities for dialogue, cooperation, and the development of mutual trust.

One example of a successful joint project is the establishment of bilingual schools where Israeli and Palestinian children study together. By sharing classrooms and learning spaces, children from both communities are exposed to different perspectives, cultures, and traditions. This exposure helps break down stereotypes, prejudice, and fear, fostering empathy and understanding from an early age.

Another initiative that has shown promise is the joint management of shared resources, such as water or agricultural land. By working together to address shared challenges, Israeli and Palestinian farmers can find sustainable solutions that benefit both sides. This collaborative approach not only promotes economic development but also builds relationships and trust between communities.

Furthermore, joint cultural events and artistic collaborations can also play a significant role in creating bridges between Israelis and Palestinians. Music, art, and theater have the power to transcend political boundaries and touch people's hearts. By organizing joint concerts, exhibitions, or theater productions, artists from both communities can showcase their talents and promote a message of unity and coexistence.

It is important to note that joint projects and initiatives alone cannot solve the complex issues of the Israel and Palestinian conflict. However, they serve as a steppingstone towards peace by creating spaces for dialogue, fostering empathy, and building trust. By engaging individuals from all social classes, including youth, educators, artists, and community leaders, joint projects have the potential to create a ripple effect that can transform the dynamics of the conflict.

Creating joint projects and initiatives is an effective strategy for promoting peace in the Israel and Palestinian conflict. By bringing together individuals from both sides, joint projects foster understanding, cooperation, and trust. Whether in education, agriculture, or the arts, these initiatives provide opportunities for dialogue and empathy, paving the way towards a future of peaceful coexistence.

ENCOURAGING CROSS-CULTURAL EXCHANGES AND INTERACTIONS

In a world that is increasingly interconnected, fostering cross-cultural exchanges and interactions is more important than ever. This subchapter explores the significance of promoting such exchanges specifically in the context of the Israel and Palestinian conflict. By applying the Zero-Violent-Conflict- Free Model, we aim to create peace in an already tense environment.

Cross-cultural exchanges provide a platform for individuals from divergent backgrounds to come together, share their experiences, and develop a deeper understanding of one another. These interactions help break down stereotypes and prejudices that often fuel conflict. By encouraging dialogue and empathy, we can build bridges between communities and pave the way for peaceful coexistence.

One essential aspect of cross-cultural exchanges is creating opportunities for people to engage in joint activities and projects. By working together towards a common goal, individuals can develop trust and build relationships based on mutual respect. This subchapter explores innovative initiatives that have successfully brought Israelis and Palestinians together, such as joint eco-tourism ventures, cultural festivals, and sports events. These activities foster a sense of unity and provide a glimpse of the shared humanity that transcends political differences.

Furthermore, this subchapter highlights the role of education in promoting cross-cultural exchanges. By integrating peace education into school curricula, we can nurture the next generation of peacebuilders. This entails teaching children about the history, culture, and narratives of both Israelis and Palestinians, fostering understanding and empathy from an early age. Additionally, it is crucial to provide opportunities for students to engage in joint educational programs, where they can interact with peers from different backgrounds and develop cross-cultural friendships.

The subchapter also addresses the significance of creating safe spaces for dialogue and reconciliation. It explores the role of community centers, NGOs (Non-Governmental

Organizations), and grassroots organizations in facilitating meaningful conversations between Israelis and Palestinians. By providing a neutral and supportive environment, these spaces allow individuals to share their perspectives, voice their concerns, and work towards finding common ground.

Encouraging cross-cultural exchanges and interactions is not without challenges, especially within a conflict-ridden environment. However, by embracing the principles of the Zero-Violence Conflict-Free Model, we can create a foundation for lasting peace. This subchapter offers practical suggestions and real-life examples to inspire individuals of all ages to become active participants in the journey towards peace in Israel and Palestine.

CHAPTER 6: TRANSFORMING CONFLICT THROUGH NON-VIOLENT MEANS

NON-VIOLENT RESISTANCE AND CIVIL DISOBEDIENCE

Non-violent resistance and civil disobedience have long been powerful tools utilized by individuals and communities to create positive change in society. In the context of the Israel and Palestinian conflict, these strategies offer a unique approach to bring about peace in an already tense environment.

Non-violent resistance is a method of protest that emphasizes peaceful means of expressing discontent and challenging injustice. It involves actions such as peaceful demonstrations, boycotts, strikes, and sit-ins. Unlike violent methods, non-violent resistance seeks to appeal to the moral conscience of those in power, aiming to change hearts and minds rather than inflict harm. This approach has been proven effective throughout history, from Mahatma Gandhi's movement in India to Martin Luther King Jr.'s civil rights struggle in the United States, to Kenule Beeson Saro-Wiwa, founder of MOSOP (Movement for the Survival of the Ogoni People), Nigeria.

Civil disobedience, on the other hand, is a deliberate violation of laws or regulations deemed unjust or oppressive. It involves acts of non-compliance, such as refusal to pay taxes, peaceful occupation of government buildings, or symbolic gestures like the salt march led by Gandhi. By intentionally breaking the law, civil disobedience challenges the legitimacy of oppressive systems and raises awareness of the injustices faced by a particular group or community.

In the Israel and Palestinian conflict, the application of non-violent resistance and civil disobedience offers a transformative approach to break the cycle of violence and build lasting peace. Instead of resorting to armed struggle or retaliatory actions, individuals and communities can engage in peaceful methods to express their grievances and demand justice.

Through non-violent resistance, Palestinians and Israelis can come together to organize joint protests, advocating for an end to the occupation, the right to self-determination, and the creation of an independent and viable Palestinian state. By promoting unity and solidarity, this approach can challenge the divisive narratives that perpetuate the conflict and create a shared vision for peace.

Civil disobedience can also be a powerful tool to challenge the policies and regulations that contribute to the ongoing tension. By refusing to comply with unjust laws, both Palestinians and Israelis can draw attention to the discriminatory practices they face and advocate for change. This can include actions such as refusing to serve in the military or participating in illegal settlements.

Non-violent resistance and civil disobedience offer a way forward in the Israel and Palestinian conflict, allowing individuals and communities to actively engage in creating peace. By adopting the zero- violent-conflict-free model, both sides can work together to build a just and inclusive society, based on mutual respect, understanding, and equality. It is through these peaceful means that a sustainable and lasting peace can be achieved, breaking the cycle of violence that has plagued the region for far too long.

PEACE EDUCATION AND CONFLICT RESOLUTION TRAINING

Peace education and conflict resolution training are essential components in creating lasting peace in any society, particularly in environments that are already tense and rife with conflict. In the context of the Israel and Palestinian conflict, these tools are crucial for breaking the cycle of violence and fostering understanding and empathy between the two sides.

The Zero-Violence Conflict-Free Model, as outlined in this book, provides a comprehensive framework for peacebuilding that focuses on nonviolent strategies and techniques. It emphasizes the importance of education and training to transform the mindsets of individuals and communities, and to promote a culture of peace.

Peace education is not limited to schools and formal educational institutions; it should be accessible to people of all ages. By educating individuals about the root causes of violence and conflict, as well as the principles of nonviolence, they can gain a deeper understanding of the consequences of their actions and the value of peaceful coexistence. Peace education helps individuals develop critical thinking skills, empathy, and the ability to resolve conflicts peacefully.

Conflict resolution training, on the other hand, equips individuals with practical skills and strategies to manage and resolve conflicts in a nonviolent manner. This training emphasizes active listening, effective communication, negotiation, and mediation techniques. By providing people with these tools, they are empowered to address conflicts constructively and find mutually beneficial solutions.

In the context of the Israel and Palestinian conflict, peace education and conflict resolution training can play a pivotal role in bridging the divide between the two sides. By bringing together individuals from both communities, these programs can foster dialogue, understanding, and empathy. They can help challenge stereotypes and prejudices and create a safe space for open and honest conversations.

Furthermore, peace education and conflict resolution training can also address the needs of individuals who have been directly affected by the conflict, such as victims of violence or refugees. By providing them with the necessary tools to heal, reconcile, and rebuild their lives, these programs contribute to the overall peacebuilding efforts in the region.

In conclusion, peace education and conflict resolution training are essential components in creating peace in an already tense environment such as the Israel and Palestinian conflict. By educating individuals of all ages and providing them with practical skills, we can break the cycle of violence and build a sustainable and peaceful future for all.

GRASSROOTS MOVEMENTS AND COMMUNITY ORGANIZING

Grassroots movements and community organizing play a crucial role in creating peace in tense environments, such as the Israel and Palestinian conflict. In this subchapter, we will explore how these methods can be applied to break the cycle of violence and foster understanding and cooperation between the two communities.

Community organizing is a powerful tool that enables individuals to come together and work towards a common goal. It involves mobilizing people at the local level, empowering them to voice their concerns, and collectively taking action. Grassroots movements, on the other hand, are driven by individuals who are deeply committed to a cause and strive to create change from the bottom up.

In the context of the Israel and Palestinian conflict, grassroots movements and community organizing can provide a platform for dialogue, reconciliation, and mutual understanding. By bringing people from both sides of the conflict together, these initiatives can humanize the "enemy" and help break down the barriers that perpetuate violence.

One effective approach is the Zero-Violence Conflict-Free Model, which advocates for nonviolent means to resolve conflicts and create sustainable peace. This model emphasizes the power of community organizing and grassroots movements by encouraging individuals to take responsibility for their actions and work towards conflict resolution through peaceful means.

Community organizing efforts can involve activities such as peace marches, joint educational programs, cultural exchanges, and dialogue sessions. These initiatives provide opportunities for people from different backgrounds to engage in face-to-face conversations, share their stories, and find common ground. By fostering empathy and understanding, grassroots movements can build bridges between communities and promote coexistence.

Moreover, grassroots movements and community organizing can also put pressure on political leaders and policymakers to prioritize peacebuilding efforts. Through public demonstrations, advocacy campaigns, and lobbying, these movements can create a groundswell of support for peaceful resolutions and encourage policymakers to take concrete steps towards resolving the conflict.

In conclusion, grassroots movements and community organizing are essential tools in the pursuit of peace in tense environments like the Israel and Palestinian conflict. By bringing people together, fostering dialogue, and putting pressure on policymakers, these initiatives can contribute to breaking the cycle of violence and creating a sustainable and peaceful future for all. It is through the collective efforts of individuals of all ages that we can make a significant impact and pave the way for a harmonious coexistence in the region.

CHAPTER 7: PROMOTING RECONCILIATION AND HEALING

RESTORATIVE JUSTICE APPROACHES

Restorative justice approaches offer a unique and transformative way of addressing conflicts and promoting peace in tense environments such as the Israel and Palestinian conflict. Restorative justice focuses on repairing the harm caused by conflict through dialogue, empathy, and understanding, rather than solely relying on punitive measures (Pointer, 2021). These approaches are explored and applied to the specific context of the Israel and Palestinian conflict.

Restorative justice approaches recognize the importance of acknowledging the needs and perspectives of all parties involved in a conflict. By providing a safe and inclusive space for dialogue, individuals and communities can actively participate in the resolution process. This allows for the development of a shared understanding of the root causes of the conflict and the impact it has had on all sides. Through this process, empathy and compassion can be fostered, leading to a greater likelihood of long-term reconciliation.

One key aspect of restorative justice approaches is the focus on repairing the harm caused by the conflict. This goes beyond punishment and seeks to promote healing and restoration for both individuals and communities. This can be achieved through a variety of means, such as facilitated dialogues, victim-offender mediation, and community conferences. By actively involving all stakeholders in the process, restorative justice approaches empower individuals to take responsibility for their actions and contribute to the rebuilding of trust and peace.

The application of restorative justice approaches to the Israel and Palestinian conflict is particularly relevant due to the deep-rooted animosity and historical grievances between the two parties. By adopting the Zero-Violence Conflict-Free Model, as outlined in this book, the potential for transformative change is immense. This model emphasizes the importance of non-violent communication, conflict resolution, and community engagement. By incorporating restorative justice approaches into this model, it becomes possible to address the underlying causes of the conflict and create a sustainable framework for peace.

Restorative justice approaches provide a powerful framework for addressing conflicts and promoting peace in tense environments such as the Israel and Palestinian conflict. By focusing on repairing harm, fostering empathy, and actively involving all stakeholders, restorative justice offers a transformative alternative to punitive measures. The application of these approaches, as explored in this book, has the potential to create lasting peace in an already tense environment.

TRUTH AND RECONCILIATION PROCESS

In the pursuit of lasting peace, one must confront the painful realities of the past. Truth and reconciliation processes have proven to be powerful tools in healing divided societies and fostering understanding and empathy among conflicting parties. This subchapter explores the significance of truth and reconciliation processes within the context of the Israel and Palestinian conflict and how they can be effectively applied using the Zero-Violence Conflict-Free Model.

Truth and reconciliation processes aim to uncover the truth about past atrocities and human rights abuses, promote accountability, and facilitate healing and reconciliation (United States Institute of Peace, n.d). They provide a platform for victims and perpetrators to share their experiences, acknowledge the pain inflicted, and seek forgiveness. By embracing these processes, societies can break free from the cycle of violence and work towards building a peaceful coexistence.

In the case of the Israel and Palestinian conflict, truth and reconciliation processes can play a vital role in bridging the divide between the two communities. The decades-long conflict has left deep scars and grievances on both sides, making the need for truth and reconciliation paramount. By acknowledging the suffering experienced by

Palestinians and Israelis alike, these processes can foster understanding and empathy, leading to a more inclusive and comprehensive peace.

The Zero-Violence Conflict-Free Model offers a unique approach to implementing truth and reconciliation processes in the Israel and Palestinian context. By employing a non-violent and cooperative framework, the model encourages open dialogue and mutual respect. It emphasizes the importance of active listening and empathetic understanding, creating a safe space for all parties involved to share their perspectives without fear of reprisal or judgment.

Moreover, the Zero-Violence Conflict-Free Model highlights the significance of youth involvement in truth and reconciliation processes. By engaging young people from both communities, the model seeks to break the cycle of inherited hatred and mistrust. It empowers the next generation to become agents of change, fostering a culture of peace and understanding that can transcend generations.

Truth and reconciliation processes are essential components of any peacebuilding endeavor, particularly in the Israel and Palestinian conflict. By applying the Zero-Violence Conflict-Free Model, these processes can become catalysts for healing, forgiveness, and a shared vision of peace. The involvement of all ages, particularly the youth, is crucial to ensure a sustainable and inclusive peace that will endure for generations to come.

PSYCHOLOGICAL SUPPORT AND TRAUMA HEALING PROGRAMS

Psychosocial support and trauma healing programs play a vital role in addressing the deep-rooted conflicts and violence that have plagued the

Israel and Palestinian region for decades. In the midst of such a tense environment, it is crucial to provide individuals of all ages with the necessary tools and resources to heal from the psychological and emotional wounds inflicted by violence and conflict.

These programs aim to create a safe space for individuals to share their experiences, express their emotions, and rebuild their lives. They offer a range of therapeutic activities, including individual and group counseling, art therapy, music therapy, and storytelling, among others. Through these interventions, individuals are encouraged to explore their feelings, confront their fears, and develop healthy coping mechanisms.

One of the primary objectives of psychosocial support and trauma healing programs is to empower individuals to break free from the cycle of violence that has plagued their lives. By addressing the psychological scars of conflict, these programs enable individuals to regain a sense of control and agency over their own lives. They help individuals develop resilience, enhance their self-esteem, and foster a sense of hope for a peaceful future.

These programs also play a crucial role in fostering reconciliation and understanding between different communities affected by the conflict. By bringing individuals from diverse backgrounds together in a supportive environment, they create opportunities for dialogue, empathy, and mutual respect. Through shared experiences and stories, individuals can begin to understand the perspectives of others and work towards building bridges of peace.

Moreover, psychosocial support and trauma

healing programs provide a foundation for sustainable peacebuilding efforts in the region. By healing individuals on a personal level, these programs contribute to the overall healing of communities and the society at large (Appleton, 2001). They help break the cycle of violence by addressing the underlying trauma that fuels conflict, promoting peaceful coexistence, and facilitating the development of a culture of peace.

Psychosocial support and trauma healing programs are essential components of the Zero-Violence Conflict-Free Model for peace in Israel and Palestine. By providing individuals of all ages with the necessary support and resources to heal from the psychological wounds of conflict, these programs pave the way for reconciliation, understanding, and sustainable peace in a tense and volatile environment.

CHAPTER 8: SUSTAINING PEACE AND PREVENTING RELAPSE

ESTABLISHING MECHANISMS FOR CONFLICT PREVENTION AND EARLY WARNING

In the pursuit of peace in the highly volatile region of Israel and Palestine, it is crucial to establish effective mechanisms for conflict prevention and early warning. These mechanisms enable the identification of potential conflicts before they escalate into violence, allowing for timely intervention and resolution. In this subchapter, we will explore the significance of such mechanisms and how they can be applied using the Zero-Violence Conflict-Free Model.

Conflict prevention is an essential aspect of

building sustainable peace. By identifying and addressing the root causes of conflicts, we can create an environment conducive to peaceful coexistence. This requires a comprehensive understanding of the underlying issues and the ability to anticipate potential triggers. By establishing mechanisms for conflict prevention, we can proactively address these triggers and work towards de-escalation.

Early warning systems play a vital role in conflict prevention (United Nations OHCHR, 2023). These systems involve gathering and analyzing data from various sources to identify emerging conflicts. This includes monitoring social media, local news, and community feedback. By utilizing advanced technologies and data analysis techniques, we can detect patterns and trends that indicate an increased risk of violence. Early warning systems empower stakeholders with the knowledge and information necessary to take preventive action (Deleersnyder & Batult, 2021).

The Zero-Violence Conflict-Free Model offers a unique approach to conflict prevention and early warning in the context of the Israel and Palestinian conflict. By creating a network of local peace ambassadors, the model establishes a grassroots system for monitoring and reporting potential conflicts. These peace ambassadors, representing diverse communities, serve as the eyes and ears on the ground, reporting any signs of tension or violence.

Additionally, the model utilizes modern technologies to enhance early warning capabilities. Using social media analytics, satellite imagery, and data-driven algorithms, the model can identify emerging conflicts with greater accuracy and speed. By combining these technological advancements with the insights provided by local peace ambassadors, the Zero-Violence Conflict-Free Model creates a comprehensive early warning system.

Establishing mechanisms for conflict prevention and early warning is a critical step towards peace in the Israel and Palestinian conflict. By utilizing the Zero-Violence Conflict-Free Model, we can proactively address the root causes of conflicts and prevent their escalation. This approach empowers individuals and communities to play an active role in maintaining peace, fostering a sense of ownership and responsibility for the well-being of their society.

The establishment of mechanisms for conflict prevention and early warning is of utmost importance in the pursuit of peace in the Israel and

Palestinian conflict. By incorporating the principles of the Zero-Violence Conflict-Free Model, we can create a sustainable framework that promotes peace, harmony, and understanding in this tense environment. Through the collaboration of individuals, communities, and advanced technologies, we can break the cycle of violence and pave the way for a peaceful future.

STRENGTHENING INSTITUTIONS AND GOVERNANCE STRUCTURES

To achieve peace in a tense environment such as the Israel and Palestinian conflict, it is crucial to focus on strengthening institutions and governance structures. This subchapter delves into the significance of building robust institutions and governance mechanisms as part of the Zero-Violent- Conflict-Free Model for Peace in Israel and Palestine.

In any conflict-ridden region, the presence of strong institutions is vital for establishing lasting peace. Institutions act as the pillars of governance, providing stability, accountability, and effective decision- making. By strengthening institutions, we can create a solid foundation for peace and ensure that conflicts are resolved through peaceful means rather than resorting to violence.

One of the key aspects of strengthening institutions is promoting good governance. This involves enhancing transparency, accountability, and the rule of law. Good governance ensures that the rights and needs of all individuals, regardless of their background, are protected and addressed. It fosters a sense of trust and confidence in the institutions, reducing the likelihood of resorting to violence as a means of addressing grievances.

Furthermore, empowering local communities and promoting participatory governance is crucial. By involving communities in decision-making processes, individuals feel a sense of ownership and responsibility towards their society. This inclusivity helps build trust between distinct groups and encourages cooperation, thereby reducing tensions and conflicts.

Another essential aspect of strengthening institutions is investing in education and capacity-building. Education plays a pivotal role in shaping the mindset of individuals and fostering a culture of peace. By promoting education that emphasizes tolerance, understanding, and respect for diversity, we can lay the groundwork for a peaceful coexistence.

Additionally, it is vital to address corruption and promote integrity within institutions. Corruption erodes public trust and weakens the effectiveness of governance structures. By implementing robust anti- corruption measures and promoting transparency, we can ensure that institutions are accountable and serve the best interests of the people.

In conclusion, strengthening institutions and governance structures is an integral part of the Zero- Violent-Conflict-Free Model for Peace in Israel and Palestine. By focusing on good governance, participatory decision-making, education, and addressing corruption, we can create a conducive environment for peace to flourish. It is through these efforts that we can break the cycle of violence and pave the way for a peaceful and prosperous future for all ages in Israel and Palestine.

INTERNATIONAL INVOLVEMENT AND SUPPORT IN MAINTAINING PEACE

International involvement and support play a crucial role in maintaining peace in conflict-ridden regions such as Israel and Palestine. The complexities of this conflict demand a multifaceted approach, involving diplomatic negotiations, economic aid, and peacekeeping efforts. In this subchapter, we will explore the importance of international involvement and support in creating peace in an already tense environment, focusing on the application of the Zero-Violence Conflict-Free Model to the Israel and Palestinian conflict.

At the heart of international involvement lies diplomatic negotiations. The conflict between Israel and Palestine is deeply rooted in historical, religious, and territorial disputes. Achieving a lasting peace requires the engagement of international mediators, who can facilitate dialogue and bridge the gap between the two parties. The involvement of international actors, such as the United Nations, the European Union, and the United States, can provide the necessary impartiality and expertise to guide the negotiation process.

Furthermore, economic aid plays a critical role in maintaining peace. Socioeconomic disparities and limited access to resources fuel tensions and grievances. International support in the form of economic assistance can help alleviate poverty, promote development, and create opportunities for both Israelis and Palestinians. By addressing the underlying economic issues, international involvement can contribute to long-term stability and peaceful coexistence.

Peacekeeping efforts also form an integral

part of international involvement. International peacekeeping forces, such as the United Nations Peacekeeping Missions, can help monitor ceasefires, prevent violence, and build trust between the conflicting parties. Their presence provides a sense of security and reassurance, reducing the likelihood of renewed hostilities.

The application of the Zero-Violence Conflict-Free Model to the Israel and Palestinian conflict offers a unique approach to peacebuilding. This model emphasizes the importance of nonviolent strategies, conflict resolution, and dialogue. By adopting this model, international actors can promote peaceful alternatives to violence, encourage reconciliation, and foster a culture of understanding and respect.

In conclusion, international involvement and support are vital in maintaining peace in the Israel and Palestinian conflict. Diplomatic negotiations, economic aid, and peacekeeping efforts all contribute to the creation of a peaceful environment. By applying the Zero-Violence Conflict-Free Model, international actors can offer innovative strategies to resolve this long-standing conflict. Regardless of age, it is crucial for all individuals to understand the significance of international involvement and support in creating peace and strive for a better future in this tense environment.

CHAPTER 9: EVALUATING THE ZERO-VIOLENCE CONFLICT-FREE MODEL

ASSESSING THE IMPACT OF THE MODEL IN ISRAEL AND PALESTINE

Amid ongoing tensions and conflicts between Israel and Palestine, finding a sustainable path toward peace seems like an insurmountable challenge. However, in this book, a groundbreaking approach is explored, offering hope for a peaceful resolution.

This subchapter delves into the assessment of the impact the Zero-Violence Conflict-Free Model could have on the Israel and Palestinian conflict. By applying this model, which focuses on creating peace in a tense environment, a new perspective is offered to all ages, regardless of their background or beliefs.

The first step in assessing the impact of the model is to understand its core principles. The Zero- Violent-Conflict-Free Model emphasizes the power of dialogue, empathy, and understanding. It encourages both sides to listen and engage in constructive conversations, fostering an environment where violence is replaced by peaceful resolutions.

The model in Israel and Palestine could have a significant impact on the attitudes and perceptions of individuals from both sides. By encouraging dialogue and empathy, people may begin to recognize the humanity in each other, breaking down the barriers that have perpetuated the conflict for decades. This change in mindset tends to lay a foundation for peaceful coexistence and paves the way for long-lasting peace.

Additionally, the model first proposed to resolve the conflict between fence line communities and multinational oil exploring companies may prove effective in reducing violent incidents between Israelis and Palestinians. Through education, community-building initiatives, and conflict resolution programs, the model promotes a shift towards non-violent responses to disagreements. This may lead to a noticeable decrease in violence, providing hope for a future where conflicts can be resolved peacefully.

Moreover, the model's impact could extend beyond the immediate conflict zone. It will inspire similar initiatives around the world, demonstrating its universal applicability. By sharing success stories and lessons learned from implementing the model in Israel and Palestine, other regions experiencing conflicts can adapt and adopt these approaches, fostering peace on a global scale.

The assessment of the impact of the Zero-Violence Conflict-Free Model in Israel and Palestine would reveal a promising path toward peace. By emphasizing dialogue, empathy, and non- violence, this model could shift attitudes, reduce violence, and inspire similar initiatives worldwide. It offers hope to all ages, regardless of their background or beliefs, that a peaceful resolution to the Israel and Palestinian conflict is indeed possible.

LESSONS LEARNED AND BEST PRACTICES FOR FUTURE APPLICATIONS

In the face of one of the longest-running conflicts in history, the Israel and Palestinian conflict, the search for a sustainable and lasting peace seems like an insurmountable task.

However, through the groundbreaking Zero-Violence Conflict-Free Model, there is hope for creating peace in this already tense environment. This subchapter aims to highlight the valuable lessons learned and best practices for future applications to pave the way for a peaceful resolution.

One of the key lessons learned from the Zero-Violence Conflict-Free Model is the importance of fostering mutual understanding and empathy. Both sides of the conflict have deeply ingrained narratives and perspectives that perpetuate the cycle of violence. By creating spaces for dialogue and encouraging open-mindedness, individuals from both sides can begin to understand each other's struggles, fears, and aspirations. Such understanding can help break down the barriers that fuel hostility and create a more conducive environment for peace.

Another crucial lesson is the power of education and grassroots initiatives. Peace-building efforts must start from the ground up, involving the youth, educators, and community leaders. By integrating peace education into school curricula and promoting cultural exchanges, future generations can be equipped with the necessary tools to reject violence and embrace peaceful coexistence. This grassroots approach ensures that the foundations for peace are solid and sustainable, as it nurtures a generation that values empathy, tolerance, and dialogue.

Furthermore, the Zero-Violence Conflict-Free Model emphasizes the significance of international cooperation and mediation. The involvement of impartial third-party mediators can help facilitate negotiations and bridge the gaps between conflicting parties. International actors play a crucial role in providing support, resources, and expertise to facilitate dialogue, build trust, and ensure the implementation of peace agreements.

Lastly, building on the best practices of previous peace-building initiatives, it is crucial to address the root causes of the conflict. Socioeconomic inequalities, access to resources, and the question of land ownership are deeply intertwined with the Israel and Palestinian conflict. By addressing these underlying issues and ensuring equitable and sustainable development for all parties involved, the chances of a lasting peace can be significantly enhanced.

The lessons learned and best practices outlined in this subchapter provide a roadmap for creating peace in the Israel and Palestinian conflict. By fostering mutual understanding, promoting grassroots initiatives, encouraging international cooperation, and addressing underlying issues, the Zero-Violence Conflict-Free Model offers hope for a future of peaceful coexistence. It is imperative that individuals of all ages, from all social classes, embrace these lessons and work together towards a better future for Israel and Palestine.

POTENTIAL CHALLENGES AND LIMITATIONS OF THE MODEL

While the Zero-Violence Conflict-Free Model holds great promise for creating peace in the Israel and Palestinian conflict, it is important to acknowledge the potential challenges and limitations that may arise when implementing this model in such a tense environment. Understanding these challenges will allow us to develop strategies to overcome them and maximize the success of the model.

One of the main challenges is the deeply rooted historical and cultural animosity between the Israeli and Palestinian communities. Decades of conflict, violence, and mistrust have created a significant barrier to peace. It will be a challenge to convince both sides to put aside their grievances and work towards a common goal. Building trust and fostering empathy between the two communities will be a crucial step in overcoming this challenge.

Another limitation of the model is the presence of extremist groups who thrive on violence and perpetuate the conflict. These groups may view the Zero-Violence Conflict-Free Model as a threat to their ideologies and agendas. Their resistance and potential acts of sabotage could pose significant challenges to the implementation and success of the model. It will be essential to address and neutralize the influence of extremist groups through counter-narratives, education, and targeted intervention.

Additionally, the political landscape and the involvement of external actors can complicate the implementation of the model. The Israel and Palestinian conflict have garnered international attention and involvement, with various countries and organizations supporting different sides. Negotiating a peaceful resolution amidst these complex dynamics will require skilled diplomacy and a commitment to inclusivity and fairness.

Furthermore, the socioeconomic disparities between the Israeli and Palestinian communities may present a challenge to the model. Addressing issues of inequality and ensuring equal access to resources and opportunities will be essential for creating sustainable peace. This will require comprehensive economic development plans that prioritize the well-being of all individuals in the region.

Lastly, sustaining long-term peace will require ongoing commitment and vigilance. The Zero-Violent- Conflict-Free Model is not a quick fix, but a continuous process that demands consistent effort and dedication from all parties involved. Overcoming complacency, maintaining dialogue, and adapting strategies as new challenges arise will be imperative for the success of the model.

While the Zero-Violence Conflict-Free Model offers a promising approach to peace in the Israel and Palestinian conflict, it is essential to recognize and address the potential challenges and limitations that may arise. By actively working to overcome historical animosities, addressing extremist influences, navigating complex political dynamics, tackling socioeconomic disparities, and maintaining long-term commitment, we can maximize the potential of the model and create a lasting peace in this tense environment.

CHAPTER 10: CONCLUSION

RECAP OF KEY FINDINGS AND INSIGHTS

In this subchapter, we will summarize the key findings and insights thus far in this book. This book provides a comprehensive analysis of the Israel and Palestinian conflict and presents a groundbreaking model for creating peace in an already tense environment.

One of the key findings of this book is the recognition that violence perpetuates a vicious cycle, leading to further aggression and retaliation. The author argues that breaking this cycle requires a shift towards a Zero-Violence Conflict-Free Model. This model emphasizes the importance of nonviolent communication, dialogue, and conflict resolution techniques to de-escalate tensions.

The book also highlights the critical role of education in creating a culture of peace. By promoting empathy, understanding, and tolerance among the younger generations, we can pave the way for a peaceful future. There are practical strategies for incorporating peace education in schools and communities, encouraging dialogue, and fostering mutual respect.

Moreover, the book emphasizes the importance of inclusivity and the involvement of all stakeholders in the peace process. It stresses that peace cannot be achieved unilaterally but requires the active participation and engagement of both Israelis and Palestinians. There is ample demonstratable effectiveness of inclusive peacebuilding efforts.

Another key insight is the need for international support and cooperation. The book argues that the international community has a crucial role to play in facilitating peace negotiations, providing resources, and promoting dialogue between the conflicting parties. It highlights the importance of diplomatic efforts and the establishment of regional partnerships to address the root causes of the conflict and find sustainable solutions.

Furthermore, there is emphasis on the power of grassroots movements and civil society in driving positive change. They highlight the efforts of various organizations and individuals who have actively worked towards peace, providing hope and inspiration for all ages.

In conclusion, "Breaking the Cycle: The Zero-Violence Conflict-Free Model for Peace in Israel and Palestine" offers a comprehensive analysis of the Israel and Palestinian conflict and presents a model for creating peace in an already tense environment. It highlights the importance of nonviolent communication, education, inclusivity, international cooperation, and grassroots movements in breaking the cycle of violence. It is a must-read for all ages, especially those interested in creating peace in the Israel and Palestinian conflict and applying the Zero-Violence Conflict-Free Model.

CALL TO ACTION FOR INDIVIDUALS AND COMMUNITIES

In a world riddled with violence and conflict, it is imperative for individuals and communities to step up and actively work towards creating peace. Nowhere is this need more urgent than in the tense environment of the Israel and Palestinian conflict. The time has come for all ages to unite and embrace the Zero-Violence Conflict-Free Model as a powerful tool for fostering peace in this region.

Creating peace in an already tense

environment requires a collective effort from individuals and communities alike. Each one of us has a role to play in breaking the cycle of violence and transforming this conflict into a peaceful coexistence. It is not enough to simply hope for peace; we must act.

First, individuals must examine their own biases and prejudices. We must recognize that peace can only be achieved through understanding and empathy. By engaging in dialogue and actively listening to the perspectives of others, we can begin to bridge the gaps that divide us. It is crucial to challenge our own assumptions and be open to alternative viewpoints.

Communities, on the other hand, have the power to create safe spaces for dialogue and reconciliation. By organizing peace-building workshops, cultural exchanges, and interfaith events, communities can foster an atmosphere of mutual respect and understanding. These initiatives provide platforms for individuals to come together, share their experiences, and find common ground.

Education also plays a vital role in creating peace. Schools and educational institutions must incorporate peacebuilding and conflict resolution into their curricula. By teaching the principles of nonviolence and promoting cultural awareness, we can empower the next generation to become active agents of change.

Furthermore, it is crucial for individuals and communities to support organizations and initiatives dedicated to peacebuilding. By volunteering, donating, or advocating for these causes, we can contribute to the ongoing efforts towards a peaceful resolution of the Israel and Palestinian conflict.

The call to action for individuals and communities is clear: we must actively participate in the creation of peace. By examining our own biases, engaging in dialogue, organizing community events, promoting education, and supporting peace-building initiatives, we can work towards a future where violence and conflict no longer dominate the Israel and Palestinian landscape. Let us break the cycle and embrace the Zero-Violence Conflict-Free Model as a pathway to long-lasting peace. Together, we can make a difference.

HOPE FOR A PEACEFUL FUTURE

In a world filled with conflicts and tensions, the hope for a peaceful future may seem like an elusive dream. However, amidst the seemingly endless cycle of violence and hostility, there is a glimmer of hope that shines brightly in the form of the Zero-Violence Conflict-Free Model for Peace in Israel and Palestine. This model offers a fresh perspective and a practical approach to creating peace in an already tense environment.

The Israel and Palestinian conflict have long been a source of great suffering and heartache for both sides. Decades of violence, mistrust, and failed peace initiatives have left many feeling hopeless and skeptical about the possibility of a peaceful resolution. But this book, "Breaking the Cycle," challenges this despairing narrative and presents a new path towards reconciliation.

The Zero-Violence Conflict-Free Model is based on the belief that violence is not the answer to conflict resolution. It recognizes that violence only perpetuates more violence and that there must be a shift in mindset and approach in order to break this destructive cycle. This model emphasizes the importance of dialogue, empathy, and understanding as key ingredients for peace.

Addressing an audience of all ages, this book aims to inspire and educate individuals from different backgrounds and perspectives. It provides an analysis of the Israel and Palestinian conflict, delving into the historical, political, and social aspects that have contributed to the current state of affairs. By understanding the root causes of the conflict, readers are empowered to challenge preconceived notions and engage in meaningful conversations.

The book also offers practical strategies and real-life examples of how the Zero-Violence Conflict-Free Model can be applied to the Israel and Palestinian conflict. It highlights success-oriented initiatives and peace- building efforts that could be undertaken by individuals and organizations on both sides. These potential initiatives serve as a beacon of hope, demonstrating that peace is indeed possible, even in the most challenging of circumstances.

Ultimately, "Breaking the Cycle" offers a roadmap towards a peaceful future for Israel and Palestine. It encourages readers to embrace a mindset of empathy, to listen to one another's stories, and to work together towards a shared vision of peace. Through this book, all ages can find the inspiration and guidance needed to create peace in an already tense environment, and to break free from the chains of violence and conflict.

REFERENCES

Appleton, V. (2001). Avenues of Hope: Art Therapy and the Resolution of Trauma. Art Therapy: Journal of the American Art Therapy Association. 19. 10.1080/07421656.2001.10129454.

D.A.S. *et al.* (2023) *Israel-Gaza conflict through the ages: A look back and its impact on the global economy - credible news, Credible News Nigeria.* Available at: https://crediblenews.com.ng/israel-gaza-conflict-through-the-ages-a-look-back-and-its-impact-on-the-global-economy/ (Accessed: 01 January 2024).

DELEERSNYDER, A.E. & Batult, F. (2021, September). Early Warning and Conflict Prevention: can indexes play a role? Retrieved from https://fundforpeace.org/2021/09/21/early-warning-and-conflict-prevention-can-indexes-play-a-role/.

Faye, J. (2023) *The Balfour declaration and the Israeli-Palestinian conflict, Medium.* Available at: https://medium.com/@historicalgeographica/the-balfour-declaration-and-the-israeli-palestinian-conflict-1d1342f2d716 (Accessed: 01 January 2024).

Historian, T. (2023) *13 facts about Zionism, Have Fun With History*. Available at: https://www.havefunwithhistory.com/facts-about-zionism/ (Accessed: 01 January 2024).

Hu, R & Han, X. (2023). *Study on the path toward solutions for Nimbyism in China: A case study based on the qualitative comparative analysis method, Heliyon*. Available at: https://www.sciencedirect.com/science/article/pii/S2 405844023074777 (Accessed: 01 January 2024).

Interobserver (2023). Active listening skills: The key to effective communication (2023a) *interObservers*. Available at: https://interobservers.com/active-listening-skills/ (Accessed: 01 January 2024).

Pillay, V. (2006). Building Peace: Sustainable Reconciliation in Divided Societies, John Paul Lederach: book review. *Conflict Trends, 2006*(1), 55-56.

Pointer, L. (2021, August). What is "Restorative Justice" and How Does it Impact Individuals Involved in Crime? Retrieved from https://bjatta.bja.ojp.gov/media/blog/what-restorative-justice-and-how-does-it-impact-individuals-involved-crime.

Sakib, N. (2023) *The complex history of Israel's takeover of Palestine, Medium.* Available at: https://medium.com/illumination/the-complex-history-of-israels-takeover-of-palestine-129d1911cc78 (Accessed: 01 January 2024).

Staff, T.W. (2023) *Israel-Palestine: Why did the Oslo accords fail?, The week.* Available at: https://theweek.com/politics/israel-palestine-why-did-the-oslo-accords-fail (Accessed: 01 January 2024).

Travers, M. (2023) *5 lessons for all 'true empaths' to live by, from a psychologist, Forbes.* Available at: https://www.forbes.com/sites/traversmark/2023/11/15/5-lessons-for-all-true-empaths-to-live-by-from-a-

psychologist/?sh=4660f3124860 (Accessed: 01
January 2024).

United Nations OHCHR (n.d). *Conflict prevention, early
warning and security | OHCHR*. Available at:
https://www.ohchr.org/en/topic/conflict-prevention-
early-warning-and-security (Accessed: 02 January
2024).

United States Institute of Peace (no date) *Reconciliation.*
Available at: https://www.usip.org/issue-
areas/reconciliation (Accessed: 01 January 2024).

*Vescio, T. K., Sechrist, G. B., & Paolucci, M. P (2003)
Perspective taking and prejudice reduction: The
mediational role of empathy arousal and situational
attributions. European Journal of Social psychology.
33(4), 455-472.*

Wagjihash (2023) *Israel-Palestine Conflict: Understanding
the root causes and ongoing dynamics, Medium.*
Available at: https://medium.com/@wagjihash/israel-
palestine-conflict-understanding-the-root-causes-
and-ongoing-dynamics-668fbb8156d0 (Accessed:
01 January 2024).

Yorgure, C. S. (2016). Multinational Corporations and

Host Communities: Proposing the zero-violent

conflict model. Bloomington, IN: Xlibris

Zionism - meaning, definition & religious (no date)

History.com. Available at:

https://www.history.com/topics/middle-east/zionism

(Accessed: 01 January 2024).